HANDS—ON JOBS

# FISHERMEN AND FISHERWOMEN

## EMMA JONES

PowerKiDS press.

New York

Published in 2016 by The Rosen Publishing Group, Inc.
29 East 21st Street, New York, NY 10010

First Edition

Editor: Katie Kawa
Book Design: Reann Nye

Photo Credits: Cover, pp. 3–24 (background texture) Toluk/Shutterstock.com; cover (fishers) Chris Cheadle/All Canada Photos/Getty Images; p. 5 project1photography/Shutterstock.com; p. 7 (shrimper) Bloomberg/ Getty Images; p. 7 (lobster catcher) Portland Press Herald/Getty Images; p. 7 (commercial fisher) MaxFX/Shutterstock.com; p. 8 Joe Belanger/ Shutterstock.com; p. 9 ksl/Shutterstock.com; p. 10 Willyam Bradberry/ Shutterstock.com; p. 11 holbox/Shutterstock.com; p. 12 M. Cornelius/ Shutterstock.com; p. 13 Thinkstock/Stockbyte/Getty Images; p. 14 Chaikovskiy Igor/ Shutterstock.com; p. 15 David Boyer/National Geographic/Getty Images; p. 16 Brigida Soriano/Shutterstock.com; p. 17 a40757/Shutterstock.com; p. 19 (boat) EPG_EuroPhotoGraphics/Shutterstock.com; p. 19 (background) Pinkyone/Shutterstock.com; p. 20 andrej pol/Shutterstock.com; p. 21 Scott Dickerson/Design Pics/First Light/Getty Images; p. 22 bikeriderlondon/ Shutterstock.com.

Cataloging-in-Publication Data

Jones, Emma.
Fishermen and fisherwomen / by Emma Jones.
p. cm. — (Hands-on jobs)
Includes index.
ISBN 978-1-5081-4363-5 (pbk.)
ISBN 978-1-5081-4364-2 (6-pack)
ISBN 978-1-5081-4365-9 (library binding)
1. Fishers — Juvenile literature. 2. Fisheries — Juvenile literature. I. Jones, Emma. II. Title.
HD8039.F65 J66 2016
331.7'6392—d23

Manufactured in the United States of America

CPSIA Compliance Information: Batch #BW16PK: For Further Information contact Rosen Publishing, New York, New York at 1-800-237-9932

# CONTENTS

# LET'S GO FISHING!

Have you ever gone fishing with your family or friends? Fishing is fun, and it's also a popular career around the world. Fishermen and fisherwomen, who are also called fishers, work hard in all types of water to catch fish and other animals in the sea. Those animals are then sold to people for food, bait, and other uses.

Fishing is one of the oldest careers on Earth. People first caught sea creatures with their hands, and then they began to use tools, such as spears, traps, and nets. Today's fishermen and fisherwomen use the latest **technology** to catch fish.

## DIGGING DEEPER

People who've chosen a career in aquaculture, or fish farming, are different from fishers. They raise fish in a controlled setting rather than catching fish in open waters.

Anyone can go fishing, but fishing with the goal of selling what you catch has a special name. It's called commercial fishing.

# MORE THAN FISH

Fishers catch all kinds of fish. What they catch depends on their location and the season. Some examples of fish commonly caught by fishers are tuna, haddock, cod, and salmon. Fishers also catch oysters and other **mollusks**, as well as **crustaceans**, including crabs and lobsters. Each kind of animal calls for a different method of fishing, and fishers have to know which method to use.

Fishers need to study the kinds of fish or other sea creatures they want to catch. They need to know how deep in the water to put their net or trap, because different sea creatures live at different depths. They also need to know which sea creatures live in the water near them during different times of the year.

## DIGGING DEEPER

Some fishers have different job titles depending on what they catch. For example, fishers who catch crabs are sometimes called crabbers, and fishers who catch shrimp are known as shrimpers.

shrimper

lobster fisher

Fishers must follow laws that state when they can fish, what kind of sea creatures they can catch, and how many creatures they can take from the water.

commercial fisher

# TOOLS OF THE TRADE

When most people go fishing for fun, they use fishing poles or nets on land or a small boat. Some commercial fishers use poles and small nets, but they often use more advanced tools to catch more fish.

Traps called pots are often used to catch lobsters and crabs. Dragged nets called dredges help fishers catch oysters and other **shellfish**. Large nets called purse seines (SAYNZ) surround fish such as salmon and tuna. Some fishers use their hands to fish with nets. On larger boats, the nets are raised and lowered by powerful machines. Fishers must learn to operate these machines.

## DIGGING DEEPER

Purse seines are used to catch more fish around the world than any other kind of net.

purse seine

The fishing boat shown here is a trawler. This kind of boat carries a trawl, which is a large, cone-shaped net dragged through the water.

# HELPFUL TECHNOLOGY

The first fishers had few tools to help them catch enough fish to make a living. However, modern fishers are able to use the most advanced technology to help them while they work.

Fishers can now navigate, or find their way, when they're out at sea by using electronic navigation systems, such as **global positioning systems** (GPS). They also use sonar to help them find fish. To use sonar, fishers send sound waves into the water. When the waves hit an object, they bounce back as an **echo**. Sonar machines use the echoes to locate schools of fish.

## DIGGING DEEPER

Animals such as dolphins and whales use their own kind of sonar—called biosonar—to find fish in deep ocean waters.

The ability to understand and use the latest technology has become an important skill for fishers to have.

# HANDS-ON TRAINING

The best way for beginning fishers to learn how to use fishing tools is to get out on a boat and start working. Most fishers don't have much formal training. They learn on the job. Fishers often find their first job through family or friends, or they find work by asking around the docks where fishers spend their time.

Some colleges offer classes to help fishers and people who want to become fishers. These include classes in navigation, fishing gear, new technology, and vessel repair. People can also take classes in fishing safety.

## DIGGING DEEPER

A vessel is a ship or large boat. A ship is generally larger than a boat.

Fishers who operate vessels must be trained to do so. Fishing boat captains must have a **license** in order to operate their boat.

# SKILLS FOR THE SEA

Proper training and education help fishers improve certain skills, such as machine operation and navigation. However, fishers require some skills and qualities that can't be taught.

Fishers need to be physically strong. They do a lot of work with their hands, as well as a lot of heavy lifting on their vessel. Fishers should also have a lot of stamina, or the strength to keep doing things for long periods of time. Fishers often work for many hours outside. They must be able to work in all kinds of weather—from heat to rain.

## DIGGING DEEPER

Fishers are often away from home for weeks or even months at a time.

Commercial fishing isn't an easy job!
Fishers have to be tough to work in the
harsh conditions they face on the water.

# LIFE ON A FISHING VESSEL

Fishing vessels aren't the easiest places to work. Even the biggest ships have limited space. Fishers working on all kinds of vessels must be good at working with others, but it's especially important for those on smaller vessels. There's very little privacy on smaller vessels for things such as sleeping and going to the bathroom.

Food isn't always easy to make or eat on a fishing vessel, either. Much of the food taken out to sea with fishers must be able to fit in a cooler to keep it from spoiling. Fishers often eat fish because they know it's fresh.

## DIGGING DEEPER

Some fishers mend their own nets on days when they're not on the water.

Fishers live and work in close quarters. If you don't like living in small spaces, commercial fishing might not be the right career for you.

# THE DEADLIEST JOB

A fishing career is filled with adventure, but it's also filled with danger. In fact, as of 2012, fishing is the deadliest job in the United States! The highest number of deaths among U.S. fishers occurred because of **disasters** on their vessel, such as a fire or the vessel sinking. Falling overboard caused the next highest number of deaths.

Fishing vessels are often far from help when they're out on the water. It's not easy for a fisher who's hurt or sick to get to a doctor or hospital.

## DIGGING DEEPER

From 2000 to 2009, fishers who worked for one **fishery** in the northeastern United States were 37 times more likely to die on the job than a police officer!

# DANGERS AT SEA

slippery decks

large waves

stormy weather

falling overboard

broken navigation tools

rocks, reefs, and ice formations

getting tangled in fishing nets or other gear

poisonous, or deadly, fumes

Shown here are just some of the many dangers fishers face every time they go out to sea.

# SAFETY AT SEA

Because fishing is such a deadly job, fishers must do everything they can to avoid getting hurt—or worse—while they work. Some fishers practice wearing survival suits, which are also called immersion suits, in case an emergency occurs. If a fisher falls overboard, an immersion suit will keep them warm, dry, and afloat until help arrives.

In Alaska, some ships have started to carry less weight when they go out to sea. This has helped prevent capsizing, which is when a vessel turns over.

## DIGGING DEEPER

Immersion suits and other gear worn by fishers are often made in bright colors, such as red, orange, or yellow. This allows fishers to be seen in bad weather and in the water if they fall overboard.

immersion suit

Fishers often wear heavy rain coats, rubber boots, and rubber gloves to stay as dry as possible while they're on the water. This gear also helps keep them safe when working with fishing tools.

# FISHING IN YOUR FUTURE

Fishing certainly isn't a boring career. Fishers face scary storms, huge waves, and months at sea away from their loved ones. However, most fishers believe the adventures they have are worth the brushes with danger along the way. Fishers do important work. Without them, we wouldn't have fish to eat!

If a career in fishing sounds cool to you, continue to learn as much as you can about it. Ask an adult to take you on a fishing trip. Someday you might be taking long trips out to sea on a fishing vessel of your own!

# GLOSSARY

**crustacean:** An animal with several pairs of legs and a body made up of sections that are covered in a hard outer shell.

**disaster:** Something that happens suddenly and causes much suffering and loss for many people.

**echo:** The repetition of a sound that is produced when sound waves bounce off an object.

**fishery:** A part of the ocean where sea creatures are caught. Also, a business that catches and sells fish.

**global positioning system:** A radio system that uses satellites to tell you where you are and to give you directions to other places.

**license:** An official paper giving someone the right to do something.

**mollusk:** An animal that has a soft body without a backbone and that generally lives in a shell.

**shellfish:** An animal, such as a crab or an oyster, that lives in water and has a hard outer shell.

**technology:** The use of science for practical purposes.

# INDEX

# WEBSITES

Due to the changing nature of Internet links, PowerKids Press has developed an online list of websites related to the subject of this book. This site is updated regularly. Please use this link to access the list: www.powerkidslinks.com/hoj/fish